D1732965

Whispers
of the
Soul

New and Selected Poems

Patricia Greer

www.ChironPublications.com

Printed primarily in the United States of America.

ISBN 978-1-63051-992-6 paperback
ISBN 978-1-63051-993-3 hardcover
ISBN 978-1-63051-994-0 electronic

Library of Congress Cataloging-in-Publication Data

Names: Greer, Patricia, 1940- author.
Title: Whispers of the soul : new and selected poems / Patricia Greer.
Description: Asheville, N.C. : Chiron Publications, [2022] | Summary: "A
  collection of poems that range from expressions of gratitude for the
  gifts of nature, to musings about aging and the fragility of life, to
  insights about women's issues and concerns, to observations about the
  complexities of family dynamics, to reflections about writing and
  therapy."-- Provided by publisher.
Identifiers: LCCN 2021056615 (print) | LCCN 2021056616 (ebook) | ISBN
  9781630519926 (paperback) | ISBN 9781630519933 (hardcover) | ISBN
  9781630519940 (ebook)
Subjects: LCGFT: Poetry.
Classification: LCC PS3607.R476 W45 2022 (print) | LCC PS3607.R476
  (ebook) | DDC 811/.6--dc23/eng/20211124
LC record available at https://lccn.loc.gov/2021056615
LC ebook record available at https://lccn.loc.gov/2021056616

Dedication

To our grands —

Brianna, who led the way and set a high bar
Sophia, who has always had a big heart and a great game face
Matilda, whose creativity makes the world a more beautiful place
Adelaide, who has a strong sense of her authentic self
Crosby, who has an inquisitive and independent spirit
Gwendolyn, who is a unique mix of tender and tough

Cole, who never gives up
Jonas, who is driven to achieve
Jack, who is successfully following his dream
Ella, who has tenacity and a quiet strength
Lusha, who cares and wants to make a difference
Maya, who is an engaging and talented performer
Camilo, who is a strong and competitive athlete
Sienna, who is a gentle presence and an insightful observer

And to my husband, Carl, who has never stopped encouraging
    me to complete this project,
with thanks and much love ...

Table of Contents

Spindrift

How quickly they disappear,
the footprints in the sand
along the edge of the ocean.
A clear trail of my walk,
there for a moment,
and then, as the next wave ripples in,
gone.

I thought the tracks might last for a while,
a little while, at least,
to show where I have walked on this earth,
where I left an imprint,
where I made a mark.
A moment,
only.

Is it a gift
to know how fleeting it is,
how fragile
the impact we think we have made?

It reminds me
to remember,
to focus on each step as I walk it,
to enjoy the feel of the wet sand under my feet,
and the warmth of early morning sun on my shoulders,
to enjoy the sight of the never-ending ocean
and the sound of wave-rhythm
punctuated by the far-off laughter of children
and sometimes
the voice
of someone who walks with me
along the way.

It reminds me to remember,
not to look back,
not to hope for permanence,
not to wish for a kind of immortality,
not to focus on where I may or may not
have left a trace.

It reminds me
to remember
to savor
the now.

Leftovers

Balance.
It seems to be the most difficult thing
for women;
they have told me so over the years.

To find the balance:
taking care of others
and taking care of themselves.

The need for time alone,
time for creativity,
time for pondering and dreaming,
time to be.

One woman struggled with it for a long time,
even realizing that it was threatening her physical health.
How could she create such space?
How could she even believe that she should?

How to answer the needs of the world,
and especially the needs of her husband,
and have anything left over for herself?

Leftovers?
The soul has needs too.
Ignore them at your peril,
I say.

Find a way.

Two Sides

A secret life,
this one,
here.

The other one,
the outside one
is simple:
the ordinary moments
of eating a grapefruit
and going to the dentist
and waiting in line at the movie theatre.
I know how to do that one,
we all do.
And it works
well enough.

But this one
here
is where it hurts
and matters.

An Old Story

My father told the story
at his birthday party.
It was his eightieth
and we had gathered together to celebrate his day,
my mother,
my sister and I,
our husbands,
and my children.
That was our family,
all of it,
and my father told the sailboat story.

We had given him a crystal sailboat,
my husband and I,
to celebrate his lifelong love of sailing.
It was pure transparence,
all line and motion and feeling.
I had thought of writing some words
about memories of a life spent tacking into the wind
and the comforting belief of a safe harbor
at the close of day.
But I knew that my father,
at eighty,
had no wish to be reminded of the reality of endings.

And he told the sailboat story.

Our family was not always harmonious then,
he began.
Not always harmonious.

And he told the story on his birthday

in the middle of this evening
when we had worn tuxedos and silk dresses
and had drunk champagne in crystal flutes
and eaten rich food with intricate sauces
at a table set with fine china and bouquets of flowers
and had brought him special presents
and had smiled a lot
and had laughed at all the amusing anecdotes
offered up to the gaiety of the occasion.
It was all very bright and shining,
this evening,
this event,
this drama.

He told the story
of how we were on the boat for the day,
he and my mother,
my sister, about five or six,
and me, about ten or eleven.
We were on the boat,
sailing along the coast of Long Island,
and he and my mother got into an argument,
a big argument, I guess,
and my mother told my sister and me
to jump overboard
and swim to shore with her.
We were passing within sight of our beach
and I guess she was pretty angry
and I guess she figured we could make it to shore.
And we did, of course,
although it was farther
and harder

than she had realized,
especially for my five- or six-year-old sister,
and my mother had to pull her on her back most of the way.

I'm glad,
in a way,
that I learned that one could jump overboard
and swim home if one needed to.

Any time.

But I can imagine
it might have been scary to two little girls.
A mutiny,
I think my mother laughingly referred to it
later.

The issue
for me
was not so much the story itself.
The issue was the retelling of it
in the middle of the party,
the reality refashioned now
into another amusing anecdote,
part of the party decorations,
inserted into the laughter and chatter
of the evening.

And the issue
was that I laughed too
and had another sip of champagne
and thought
that it wasn't so bad after all.

It was just a story,
an old story,
safe enough now
to be told at an eightieth birthday party.
Amusing, even.
Weren't we all laughing?
Our family was not always harmonious
then,
he said.

And we all made it to shore. Unharmed.

Didn't we?

Therapy?

So he went home to his wife
and asked her,
"Do you have any dreams for your life?"

The therapist told him to do it.
So he did.
Maybe twenty years too late
or thirty,
but he's been busy, after all,
and important.

A stunned silence
answered.
Did she remember any?
Did she ever have any?
Was the question absurd
now?

Dreams need attending,
honoring,
hoping, even.

So they both went back to their corners,
their usual corners,
and carried on.

"Who needs therapy"
they thought.

For Elizabeth

She says she needs
deep silence
in order to create,
to attend,
to deepen.

So she gets up before dawn
every day
and gives it to herself,
a beautiful gift to soul,
to be treasured,
enjoyed,
honored.

But I wonder,
is it only women
who have to go to the far edges of the day
to find a little space?

Should it be this hard?

A Lesson Learned

Stewed tomatoes—
I still don't like them.

I remember,
I was four or maybe five
and I had been sitting at the table for a long time
with a plate of stewed tomatoes
in front of me.

It was the rule,
my mother said,
I had to eat them
or at least try them.
As long as I lived in their house,
she said,
I had to follow the rules.

So I decided I had to leave.

I went upstairs to pack my bag
and my mother called:
"don't take anything we gave you."
She was just trying to stop me,
I guess,
maybe in the only way she knew.

I look back at that little girl,
pleasant,
not used to disobeying the rules.
She had a good behavior chart in her room
with lots of gold stars on it.
But she decided
she had to leave.
So she took a single nickel

which I guess she had gotten from someone else
and went out the door.

She didn't get far;
she wasn't allowed to cross the street
so she didn't get far.

I don't remember how the story ended;
somehow she was back in the house.

She learned a lesson that day
but it wasn't about stewed tomatoes,
though she never ate them
again.
She learned that she could never fully trust
that things that were given were really and safely hers.
Ever.

But she learned, too, that she could leave if she wanted to,
and she has more nickels now,

and she can cross the street.

Sunday Morning Song
at a Small Chapel

The music ripped me open
and I bled
tears.

They made love to each other with their voices
and to us
and to the Lord,
and they meant it.

The burning wood ignited there
in our midst
and singed our souls
indelibly.

I could tolerate no words
afterward;
even the sound of a fly
buzzing in the chapel
was too piercing.

Absolute and awful silence
was the only
response
possible.

The Interview

Your outsides
demanded to see
my inside:
tell us the truth, you said,
tell us your truth,
and we'll tell you if it's good enough.

Such a lovely invitation,
how could I refuse?

But I've lived more than half my life, now,
and I've had cancer.
How much was I willing to turn myself inside out
for you?

Not enough, you said,
you four, comfortable in your group,
even showing off a little
for each other
as you took turns stepping into the center
of the circle.
All you have to do
is get up and dance for us,
you said.

I couldn't move.
No,
I wouldn't move.

You had something
I wanted
and I did get it.
But I still don't believe in soul work
by committee.

"Does it Still Bother You?" He Asks

She looks like an ordinary woman.

She could pass
in the land of the living
as one of them,
usually,
except for the plant.

It grows from her mouth:
an old vine thrusts brutally up her throat,
twists through her smile,
creeps over her nose and eyes.
Harsh tendrils
grab onto her face,
tangle through her hair
suck on the blood of her pulse.

Planted as seed in her body
long ago,
pushed deep into the virgin earth of her ground,
it rooted in suffocating silence.

The wound closed over
afterward
and is hardly visible
to a naked
eye.

But the vine pushed its way out
finally
closing off the throat, finally,
forcing open the mouth
in one long silent scream.

A Morning in Arizona

We've been here a week now
and we always have our morning coffee
outside
even though the air is chilly
and the sun a bit reluctant, these days.

We sit in the green of nature
and drink it in
with our daily brew.

And one day I said,
I haven't heard any doves
all week.
I miss them.
And just then
a distinctive cooing
echoed down the mountains
and through the cactus garden.

Coincidence?
Synchronicity?
Perhaps.
But I prefer to think of it as a gift,
a blessing,
a little miracle, even.

Ask and you shall receive.

Neglecting the Feminine

Shards of glass,
sharp, jagged, cruel,
pierce my head,
the pure glass of psyche
broken
and
turned against myself,
icy cold
and diamond hard.

The young feminine
thought to be dead,
deserted in a closed room
until the women came,
sisters
and daughters.
Only then
did I dare to open the door
for her.

I had neglected her
for a whole day
or a whole lifetime
because I thought I had killed her.
So great was my fear
and my shame
that I left her alone, abandoned,
closed in the room.

Body knowing is this:
words, like glass, can kill.

Or Else

I need to be messy
when I write,
and careless, in a way.

I need to scribble on scraps of paper
that can go missing,
fall behind the sofa,
get buried under layers of lists
on the desk,
blow away in the breeze.

A notebook is too direct,
intentional;
I need to sneak up on it
and pretend not to care
too much.

Or else
I would have to mean it.

Options

Little girl, about 4 years old:
I think I want to be a princess when I grow up.

Her Mom:
What does a princess do?

Little girl:
She's beautiful.

Her Mom:
But what does she do?
You can be a princess and also be a doctor or a nurse or a lawyer or
   a writer or an artist or a chef or anything you want.

Little girl:
(pause)
I think I want to take care of children.

Her Mom:
Like a teacher?

Little girl:
No. Like a Mom.

Well, she's older now,
that little girl,
and doesn't much care about princesses anymore,
though she still likes some fancy and sparkle on occasion.
Now it's all about horses,
and a dream of a ranch out west somewhere
or a center where she can give riding lessons.

She may pursue these dreams
and many others in the years ahead.
She has learned already, I think,

from her Mom and others,
that she can have many dreams in a lifetime.

Even some at the same time.

It's a good time to be a woman, I think.
Not always easy,
and definitely not perfect.
But good.

A Day

Morning spreads across the lake.
Moving mists
announce the birth
in secret
until the light pierces through
and triumphs.

Afternoon settles,
hums with insect song,
softens into cool and gentle
and tiptoes toward
evening.

Night blankets all,
challenges our senses
and our feeling of safety,
perhaps,
bringing dreams
to delight,
or mystify,
or terrify.
And we remember being little
and helpless
again.

Until morning.

Why

A woman had dreams for years
that something was wrong
in her life,
but usually she could ignore them.

Until she began to paint,
finally,
and the dreams stopped.

And then she figured it out,
sort of.

So she set up a place to make art
in an unused corner of the living room,
so the story goes,
and thought it was fine.
Good, even.

My friend told the story in her book
and I read it there
and wondered.

Why did she think that, I wondered?
Why must she fit herself
into an unused corner?
Why take only what isn't already used
by someone
or something else?
And think it's fine.
Good, even.

And then one day her husband suggested
they clear out the spare room
and make a better place for her to work.
So she did.

And felt happy.
And thought it was fine.
Good, even.

But why, I wonder,
did she need to wait
for an invitation
to claim her space.

To claim her life.

This poem was inspired by a story in Psyche's Knife by
Elizabeth Èowyn Nelson.

Early Morning

Is there anything better
than a comfortable chair
next to a small table
holding one mug of coffee
on a deck
overlooking the lake
with only the trees for company,
only the trees,

for a while?

Kindness

Three newborn mice
in a shoebox
huddled together
for warmth
and perhaps a kind of comfort.

The children had found them in the basement,
abandoned, it seemed,
unmoving.
"Are they dead," they asked?
So we put them in the shoebox
and gave them sugar water
and a slice of cheese
and a grape.
What does one give to just-born-almost-dead
mice babies?

And then they started to move a little
and sip some water
and nibble at what we hoped was mouse food.
And they lived through the night,
surprisingly.

But what does one do with a shoebox full
of baby animals
meant to live in the wild?

We set them free, soon,
and hoped.

But I had to wonder,
did our kindness benefit them
or us?

Two Daughters

It feels like only a short time ago
that I was caring for them as young children,
loving and giving of myself
as I could,
always hoping,
as any mother would,
that it was enough.

As any mother knows,
it is a gift to see something of myself in each of them,
the smile, the eyes, something in the face,
but more importantly, something in the spirit.
It is a gift to see something of myself carried forward,
something of what I believe in,
something of what I treasure.

And as any mother knows,
it is a gift to see their uniqueness,
each of them different from me and from each other,
their own styles
their own gifts
their own values and concerns.

As any mother would,
I feel sadness for their griefs
and happiness for their joys,
pride in their accomplishments
and hopes for their dreams.

It never ends, this mother caring,
even now
as they care for their own children,
and care, often, for me,
and care for the world.

Enough?

Is it enough
to sit
with paper and pencil
and invite the words?

I can only clear the space
and wait.

Perhaps that is my task,
to be the willing scribe,
attending,
in sacred silence.

Perhaps
it is
enough.

A Woman's Way

At best,
I felt patronized
by her
who has been called friend;
at worst,
I felt attacked
so subtly,
I did not know how
to defend myself.

A series of barbs
just below the level of radar,
sideways,
hidden in the laughter of convention,
piercing the soft places
left exposed.

To protect myself
I camouflaged as one of them,
joining in the abuse of the feminine:
isn't she ridiculous, I laughed,
isn't she awful?
Isn't a woman
who tries to stand up in her anger
a bitch?

Turning Fifty

The fever of fifty
burned away the outer celebration
and turned the fool's gold
into lead.

Sometimes, it seems,
lead is what is needed:
a sinker
to pull one into the greyness
of the ordinary
and the real.

Death waits
not so far along the road,
hidden at the side somewhere,
but close enough to smell
when the wind is right.

And life waits,
unfinished,
the emptiness of canvas
still cause for terror
and joy.
For one who has sniffed death
fifty is reason enough
to celebrate,
and fifty-one
to hope.

It is time to rejoice
in the dailyness.
It is time
to risk
life.

Living with Breast Cancer

This mask
that is growing on my face
comes too soon.
Who is the person in the mirror
these days?

Suddenly old,
something a little off,
the colors wrong,
a hardness
a drying up.
The leaf crackles and fades
as the tree ages.
Life pulls inward
like the scar near my breast,
the scar star
pulling all to its center,
tightening and shrinking
my world.

I do not get to choose the markings
of face
or breast.
They are gifts,
wanted
or unwanted.

A Cautionary Tale

After his Mom read him the story of "The Three Bears,"
the young boy asked
"why didn't they just lock the door"?

He's four years old
and he's pretty smart;
he hasn't lived enough years yet
to unlearn the simple truths,
to believe that it has to be all that complicated.

Well, it would ruin the story,
but that's a different issue.

So why didn't they?
And why don't we?
Sometimes boundaries are not all that hard to secure.
Why don't we take better care
of our treasures,
of ourselves?

A Young Boy

I saw him the other day
as I stood by the kitchen sink
and looked out the window.

He was young, maybe six or so,
walking to school,
cutting through the neighbor's yard,
swinging his backpack around him,
back and forth
back and forth
so earnestly,
as only a young boy would do.

If I knew his mother
I would tell her:
look away for a moment
and he'll be swinging a briefcase
with a different kind of earnestness
on a different path.

And you'll be happy for him,
and proud of him,
of course.

But once in a while you'll ache for those moments
and the sweet bitter rush of years
and the small missing piece
in your heart.

A New Year

The end of August.

Is it just me,
or does this feel like the start of a new year,
more than, say,
January 1st?

A new beginning,
all fresh and shiny,
waiting.

An old longing for sharpened no. 2 pencils
in a red pencil case.
A stack of new notebooks,
pages blank,
waiting for words and scribbles.
A backpack, a lunchbox, school shoes.
Maybe even a new outfit for the first day.

I think maybe I should treat myself to a box of crayons,
the extra-large size, all the colors, none broken yet,
and, as my youngest granddaughter would say, a "sparkly
    notebook."
And take some time to play.

Because I can't go back to the first day of school anymore,
and this may be the closest I can come to those old feelings.
Fresh and shiny and new.
Full of possibilities.

Nothing broken yet.
Not yet.

A Dream of Becoming

We work together, she and I,
she who is so close to me,
so important to me,
that I sometimes cannot see who she is
separate from me.

We work together, she and I,
in a gathering of women
outside, far away from the city.
A space has been cleared —
it is always important to prepare the place —
and we have come together.
We don't all know each other
but we are all connected
by the knowing.

We work together, she and I,
and we carve an image
from wood,
an image not yet fully formed,
a figure,
a shaping of phallic strength,
a suggestion of female mystery.
It isn't clear
if we work on one image
or two,
or if two are one.
We carve an image,
we work on it,
we do the work.
It is beautiful and pleasing,
this image becoming,
worked,

this myself
growing from a tree,
like a tree,
being held and carved and worked.

We work together, she and I,
and when we finish
we make a fire in which to place the image
to be consumed,
returned to spirit.
It is ritual.
It is right.
The image is not to be carried back
in our hands.

We work together, she and I.
It is the secret of soul making,
outside the gates of the city:
the women,
only the women,
working the piece of wood,
the treeness
of self.

Age Spots

Age spots,
they call them.
More like battle scars,
I say,
or badges of courage
or visible awards, perhaps,
for having made it this far.

This slow walk,
putting things down as I travel,
each step
now
another challenge,
another letting go,
till what is left
is distilled to the essence,
the marrow.

I have learned to savor it.
Mostly.

For Linda

She died today.

I had been given her name by the oncology staff;
she had offered
to talk to women newly diagnosed
with breast cancer,
and I had reached out to her
and we had shared stories
and cried and laughed together.

Strange how she had come back to my thoughts
these last few weeks.
I wanted to connect again
to let her know how much she helped me
back then,
when my world fell apart
a little.

So I tried to reach her,
and they told me she had died.

I hope she knows.
The sisterhood.
The battle lines.
As one falls,
another takes her place in the fight.
I feel the loss of her energy
though I hardly knew her.

I mourn her,
and she reminds me:
don't wait
to love.

Easter

He said He would meet us
in Galilee,
where it all began.
He said for us to go there
to find Him.

He would go first,
He said,
and prepare the way.
All we have to do is show up,
He said.

Sounds easy.

Ordinary Time

Before Christmas
it sometimes works:
to string hundreds of small white stars
on bare tree branches
against the darkness of the longest night,
to play the familiar music
against the silence of winter cold,
to gather family and friends
around the fire
and enjoy a kind of warmth
for a while.

After Christmas
it is darker
and colder
and more empty than before.

It is ordinary time
again.
Sometimes
I have to remind myself
to love it.

Drawing a Rune:
Protection Reversed

It reminds her
to remember:
there is no safety
finally
in anyone else.
She learned the lesson early
but she sometimes tries to forget it
and dream a new reality.

There is only the safety
within
and if that is a lonelier place,
it is, at least,
constant.

Want nothing
and you can't be held hostage
to your desires.

She uses the pain
to remember
and
deepen.

The New Year

It's early in the new year,
usually a time of shoulds,
doing more,
and better,
lists and intentions and goals.
All good,
probably.

But I wonder,
might we think about
doing less?
Might we take time,
at least a little,
to sit,
and do what looks like nothing?
Might we enjoy
the gifts of the season:
darkness and silence?

I am sometimes awake before dawn,
before the early slant of light
appears in the winter sky.
It is time
slowed
for a while.

Perhaps we are meant to hibernate
just a little,
to withdraw
and luxuriate in inner spaciousness.
Perhaps then
in that interior darkness
and silence,
we might hear the still small voice
that calls,
in the whispers of the soul.

Cold

It's always a little cold at night
and darkly quiet,
a good time to write the soul.

The fear wakes up and dances
and I watch it
twist
and weave.

I long for comfort,
a blanket of words to wrap around me
so I can feel warm
and held
and safe.

But no,
the task is calling.
I need to stay cold
to honor the truth
and summon the courage
to write it.

The Search

The search
for meaning and metaphor
continues.

I walk the beach
looking for clues:
driftwood,
odd bits of colored glass,
long damp ribbons of seaweed,
shells of spiral shapes and hidden life,
and stones worn almost smooth.

I sort through the treasures,
arranging and rearranging,
looking for connections
and patterns.

I take a stick
and scratch some shapes in the sand;
for a moment the kaleidoscope stills
and settles.
And then a bird calls
or a shadow moves
and, as I turn around,
the waves wash in
and over.

The search continues.

The Patriarchy

I have the key to this room,
this room where women stand
ready
to submit.

It is the circle of women
defiled:
they stand
in the service
of the male.
Object passes
from hand to hand
and the game continues,
woman
as object of his pleasure.

She stands
just slightly to my left
and passes me the object.
It is my turn.
Betrayed
not only by the perpetrator
but by the women,
the women who stand
together.

Chosen
to be in the circle,
seduced
by the power
of the promise
of the end of loneliness.
We have chosen
too.

I leave.
I leave
and search for others
outside the circle.
Surely there must be others
who see.
Surely there must be others
who see
what is happening
inside that room.
The men have guarded the secret
for years,
even the good men,
silenced
for years.

Persephone abducted,
deserted by the mothers.
"Where is the rage
of the mothers?"
I scream.

It is time.

Dream Words

"Too late."
The dream words woke me
and made me leave the soft rumpled pillows
and the thick down comforter
and come here to struggle
and wonder.

Is it always too late?

Even as I read a story to my granddaughter
or wash my hair
or drink a cup of coffee,
do I know?

Me and the Grands

They used to call me Grammar Grammi;
I often tried to get them to change a common grammatical
    mistake.
It's not "me and the grands," for example.
It's "the grands and I."

I had limited success.
But we had fun with it.
Two of the girls made a video about me,
in costume and with a rap sequence—
Grammar Grammi in full teaching mode,
so they said.

And one of the girls recently achieved a perfect score
on a language exam
and called, laughing,
to give me credit.

We did lots of things together when they were younger:
playground visits
and trips to the Arboretum
and ice cream runs
and shopping excursions
and art sessions
and lunch dates
and bookstore outings.

Our visits have changed since then,
at least for the older ones;
we usually meet for coffee or a meal together.
As one of the girls said, reminiscing about earlier times,
"Now we just sit and talk."

And the world has changed since then.
Once in a while I think back to Grammar Grammi
and wish that I still had advice that was so clear and certain
    and direct—
that all we had to worry about in this world now
was grammar.

Warnings

You're not supposed to look back
ever.
All the old stories tell you that.
Something about a pillar of salt
or a loved one turning away,
unable to follow.
Dire warnings,
to be sure.

But why?
What's the problem?
Eyes straight ahead
always,
they say,
like a horse wearing blinders.

So we can run faster?
So we stay focused?
So we keep moving
forward?

It seems to be some kind of bargain,
like
don't eat the apple
or else.
Or else what?
Knowledge?
Perspective?
Wisdom, even?

At what price?
Always a price to be paid.

When is it too high?

What Will It Take?

What will it take
to align my choices
more closely
with my time,
to connect
my words with my wishes,
to say no to all the things
that will clear the way
for the yes
that feeds my soul.

What will it take
to make stillness
more important than busy,
to make beauty more necessary
than food,
to make love
all.

What will it take
I asked myself,
another cancer diagnosis?

And then I got one.

Violation, According to Margeaux

Like a book,
written perhaps in a foreign language
or a code,
she has forgotten how to read
her self.

Her body remembers:
it took in the other,
intruder and treasure, both,
and cut away part of itself
to make room,
hollowed out some emptiness
within itself
for that which was different,
invader.

Chosen:
specialness and curse
together.
Object, other,
wrapped in gold threads,
dipped in shame.
History
written on the body,
remembered,
and not remembered,
worded,
and not,
deeper down
inside
underneath.

Like each of us,
she is the only witness.

Inspired by artwork titled "The Only Witness" by Margeaux Klein

Words

Words,
written,
moisten the moment.
An inner thirst
slaked,
balm
for the soul.

And then,
when I have birthed them
with struggle and pain,
I offer them to you
as part of my hiddenness,
my secret.

It honors me
to have you hold them,
listen to them,
circle the meaning
and speak it back, finally,
with a hushed tone,
and sometimes a tear
to match mine.

A Gathering of Women

It is a gathering of women.
Away from the city
outside the walls of the city
the women gather,
close to the water
high on a hill near the temple they tend,
the women gather.

They talk
together.

One of them wears red.
Perhaps she is the one who gathers them
or the one who listens
or the one who watches
or the one who is on fire with urgency
or the one who is bleeding
or the one who is about to give birth
or the one who is consumed with rage
or the one of eight
chosen.

The faces may change.

They meet from time to time
close to the water.

They stand tall
and they talk
together.

Little Deaths

I fill little scraps of paper,
endlessly,
spilling my insides out
in a rush of words,
sometimes intact,
more often bloody and bruised
and hurting.

What is the point of it all
except to try to live?

And when will I know
that I have written
all the words that live inside me?

When they stop flowing?

Or will that mean
that some have died
inside?

They Call it Transference

Like a child to her teacher,
I bring you my drawing,
timid colors crayoned hesitantly,
thin lines wavering across a small portion of the page.
"It's nothing," I tell you,
"I just scribbled it quickly,
I don't even like it, anyway."

But I had worked on it carefully
trying to do it well,
whatever that is,
trying to get it right,
whatever that is,
wanting to please you
and me
with the result.

It's a picture of you,
you see,
and a picture of me.
Can you see that?
And I know how important it is,
I can feel it,
I have finally learned to feel it.

Were my pictures intricate enough to engage your trained eye?
Then we laughed together
and you sat with me when I cried
and I knew that your brilliance
was the least important gift
you gave me.

Flattened

The year the world
shut down.

Well, it was more than a year,
and it was more than the world
that shut down.

There were lives lost
and livelihoods lost,
serious tragedies,
heart-wrenching tragedies.

And the rest of us, the lucky ones,
we hurt too.
Outside, even in winter where winter is cold,
we got together in garages with the doors open
with lawn chairs pulled inside and blankets wrapped around us
and sometimes strings of small white lights
hung across ladders and rakes and shovels
to try to summon festive.

And we were grateful
to have even this connection
with our loved ones,
not touching
hands,
but touching hearts.

And many of us
shut down inside too.
Energy went flat,
like day old ginger ale left open.
Lots of time,
nothing but time,

to write or paint or sew or work with clay,
but there was no fizz left.

And now,
are we coming out of it?
Will we go back to something we had before?
Will we create something new?
Will we heal, finally,
and reclaim what we thought of as normal?
Love and work and play, they say,
make a life.

I remember.

Will we get there?

Choices

"Irrelevant"
she said,
and then, "elderly."
She was talking about all of us,
herself included,
the four of us
gathered to share a meal
and conversation.

She's a good friend
so I paused to consider her labels.
But no,
they didn't fit for me,
or maybe I just refused to try them on.

So,
how to defy the judgments,
fly in the face of,
as they say.
Old, yes,
it's a fact.
But irrelevant and elderly
are choices,
I believe.

I can decide to stay in the world,
contribute
something,
keep moving
body and mind.

And pause more often
to contemplate,
enjoy,
give thanks and praise.
We have time
now.

We still have time
now.

A Little Too Close

She walked toward me,
a stranger,
coming a little too close,
and I put my hand up to ward her off,
to caution her back.

We were sitting outside at a small table in a small town,
eating grilled cheese sandwiches,
the specialty of this coffee shop.

We had used masks to go inside to order,
but we felt safe enough now to eat outside.

Until she approached,
a little too close.

She was just being neighborly
in a neighborly kind of town,
chatting about how good the sandwiches are
and how she likes them too
and how she comes here often to enjoy them.

And I put my hand up.

It was reflexive;
I didn't think about it,
wasn't intentional about it,
just an automatic response to try to protect myself.

But even as I did it,
I was a little appalled.

This is what we have become to each other: danger.
This is what Covid has infected us with:
fear.

It was reasonable;
I am at high risk and have to be extremely cautious
in these dangerous times.

But I was a little appalled.

It was a gentle gesture,
and I pulled it back quickly.
She may not even have noticed.

But I noticed.

Even those of us who don't get infected
may get infected.

How Many?

How many more days
do I have?

Well,
I have this one.
That's really all I know.
The question intensifies
with age
or illness,
but it's there for all of us,
haunting us
from the edges of our lives.

We ignore it,
usually.
But sometimes we hear it,
sometimes it gets louder,
demanding attention.

The truth is, though,
we all have only this one day.
For certain.
Perhaps the question we should be asking
is how we live in it,
this one miracle of a day,
how we live into it
how deeply,
intentionally,
fully.

That's the question,
isn't it?

Full

Nothing to say,
nothing to say.
I lie here in the hammock looking up at the trees,
pine, maple, birch,
needles and leaves like green gold
in the sun.
I feel full,
just beautifully full
with nothing to say

except

thank you.

Poems from *Breast Cancer, A Soul Journey*
and
*Soul Play, A Workbook to Inspire
and Guide your Soul Journey*

Speaking of Fairy Godmothers

There were thirteen of them in the kingdom,
thirteen fairy godmothers,
wise women or witches, as you wish,
but there were only twelve gold plates for the celebration.
You see the problem
already:
it is always with the uninvited guest,
the rejected aspect,
the disowned self.
Gold plates are so important, after all,
so shining and substantial.

So they each of them, the godmothers,
eleven of them in turn
gave blessings to the child,
gifts and powers and riches,
and she moved through the years,
half a lifetime and more.

And then the thirteenth spoke, out of turn.
When the thirteenth speaks
she always interrupts
where we think we are.
And there was darkness in the land.

But the twelfth had yet to be heard.
She appeared in black,
as she usually does,
skirts swirling streaks of gold,
not like the plates, though,
more like flashes of brilliant light and beckoning laughter.
She spoke softly but with sureness:
she knew all about curses and spells and antidotes
and the long forgotten art of making gold.

"It will not always be so," she said,
and quietly took her place in the circle
of women.
And it wasn't.

It's a long ago story
of gold plates and spells and falling asleep
and briars growing around
hiding, closing off, deadening.
We all sleep through it
most of the time,
and worry about the number of gold plates on the shelf,
and forget about the uninvited thirteenth
and the inevitable curse of darkness.

Until we don't.

Reasonable Limits

It is not
enough
any more
to have a room of my own;
I need the whole house empty.
The longing
grows
like cancer.

Like cancer
which grew so insistently in my breast
demanding
too much space
near my heart,
uncontainable,
the desire grows.

Womanbreast and womanheart
trained early toward the other;
I have never learned to close my ear
to the footsteps outside my door.

So what I long for is space,
room to dance naked
with no unwanted gaze,
time to sit alone
and breathe the silence.

This I have learned from cancer:
I am no longer willing
to be contained
by reasonable limits.
I want the whole house
and more.

Soul Play

Chaos may grow
out of control
in the body
of one who wants to be
spirit.
It may scream inside
the one who yearns
too urgently
for silence.

Psyche doesn't like the seesaw at rest,
one end planted firmly in the dry dirt
of the abandoned playground,
the other pointed too high
toward the gods.

A seesaw is for playing:
soul loves to be in motion,
balanced for a moment
and then flying free again,
delighting in the craziness
of the ride.

Hermes may jump suddenly on one end,
startling the unsuspecting rider perched carefully opposite,
shaking him loose,
even throwing him off.
Hades may reach up to the elevated seat,
yanking it abruptly
down,
down into his realm
of the depths.

One never knows who will enter the game
when psyche plays.
Chaos
may be exactly
what is needed.

An Inner Guide

Soul Woman,
she called herself.

We sat together for a while
outside
in silence,
and then our spirits
got up and danced together.

We lay down under a tree
on the grass
and rested
and waited.

She led me to the top of the mountain.
There was a temple there,
very old
and crumbling.
The white columns were broken off
and the weeds had grown up around it.

I wondered whose temple it was
and she answered:
this is the temple of women.
You have been worshipping at the wrong temple.

I felt her truth
with my tears
and we worked to repair the damage.

It was a place of whiteness and simplicity:
white fluted columns held up a white roof
and the sides were open to sunlight and breeze,
the blues of sky and sea,
and the greens of growing earth.

We sat on the grass
and waited
and rested.
Again.

I need time
to let the experience
seep into my bones and flesh.
This is body-knowing she is teaching me:
I must slow down my rhythms
to let it enter.

The Cancer of Silence

There are two kinds of silence
I have learned about.

In one,
an old one,
a woman stands deadly still,
a bar of iron pressed across her chest
pressed into her flesh
and the flesh grown over it
long ago
and the body grown around it
curled imperceptibly
in an almost invisible cringe.

There is another kind of silence,
much newer and without form,
the silence of remembering,
of knowing without words,
of drawing deep into the body of self
to trust there for the first time,
to stop the busyness of the dance,
to stop.
It is the silence of the earth
Embraced.

Is it the fear
or the memory
of the hot iron bar branding into her flesh
that keeps her dancing?

Getting a Mammogram

I wait in the room
while they look at the black pictures
to see if the cancer is there
still
or again.

I look out across city space
at the buildings,
rows and rows of windows
like hundreds of dead eyes,
hiding any secrets of life,
only mirroring.

I feel a part of me dead:
not only where the lump
grew
but other parts of me too
which hide the life
and only mirror.

A mirror is hard and flat.
A person
should not be.

Dead eyes
and black pictures
and mirrors.
And me.

Writing

I write to know.
It's as if I don't know
until the words come,
until the words tell me what I know.
It's not to remember, exactly,
It doesn't feel like that,
although somewhere I know
before words.

I write to see,
to take what's there, unformed,
and work it somehow
feel it and work it
like clay in my hands
and make it appear
there
where I can see it.

It feels finished
for a little while.
And then the longing arises
again,
a different kind.
It requires the other
to listen,
to touch,
to hold.

But I can never write for you.
I can only write for me
and hope.

A Woman of the Patriarchy

Her desires
lie buried under layers of
his choices.

She is disappointed,
not so much that she will never get
what she may want
but that she will never even know
what it is.
It is the way of things,
even here,
even now.

She learned long ago
not to want,
to find safety
and strength
in the killing of desire.
It is not so hard any more.

But something stays dead,
she has learned:
a little piece,
a little more each time
stays dead.

Some days she wonders
if she will find the perfect solution,
the ultimate
not
wanting.

Wording the Process

I write in pencil
so I can work the words;
like clay,
they must not harden
too soon.

One cannot write poetry at a computer.
Poetry must be made by hand,
pencil and paper,
the wood of a tree
worked.
Words written,
looked at,
listened to,
felt,
changed.

Erasures and smudges are good.
Lurches and stumbling are necessary.
This is not to be a casual stroll in the park.

December

December should be a time of waiting,
of preparing the silence,
of moving to the still point
within,
of remembering
the story and the stories
of birth
and love.

Nature teaches us how
if we listen through the noise
to the quiet.
Snow falls silently white
and makes a blanket of hush
to soften the earth.
Bare branches of maple
silhouette against the pale liquid
of winter sun
so that we may better see
the flash of scarlet bird.

The earth darkens.
It is the time of longest night
and deepest chill,
sometimes bone deep;
it moves us toward the light and warmth
of morning sun
and evening fire.

December should be a time
of following the star.
I remember the one in Bethlehem
ages old,
and I remember the one I carry near my heart:

the scar star,
stellated, they say,
focusing the pattern of my life,
pulling me to its center.

December should be a time of waiting
but I rush and flurry;
December should be a time of stillness
but the lists jangle.
There was no room at the inn;
there is no room within.
The silence of the star calls
urgently.
It is already
December.

The Seduction of Order

I want my world to be a Zen garden.
I rake the sand carefully
each morning
and place the stones
just so
in some illusion of beauty
and meaning.

And then I look away
and something is thrown in from just beyond the edges:
it splatters in the sand
and destroys the pattern.
At night
things grow from below:
they burst through
at will
crowding out the order
and the attempt at peace.

Truth
is so messy
and inconvenient.

And is the point of the garden
after all
to organize
or to ensoul?

Green for Healing

Green
for healing:
expanse of lawn,
smooth and restful;
leaves uncurling
and opening upward
toward the sun;
slender shoots
pushing through the earth
to be born
and bloom.

Life emerges again every Spring;
It's one of the things I love most
about winter.

So after cancer,
green
for healing.

Emerald power
pulling in light and energy.
Sunshine
and prayer
and green for healing.

So it can be
after
cancer.

The Web

The web
of connectedness,
random,
but patterned,
contained.
Circular,
like the rings in a tree
marking growth,
like a staircase
too close to the roots
of an old tree.

The life lines
woven fine:
a delicate structure,
but strong enough
to support.

A quietness of things,
hard stone
in a circle
almost,
and soft shells
whorled
and ancient.

Timeless and still
in the frame
of meaning,
ephemeral in form,
forever
in soul.

Rich

Riches:
the society lady on Saturday night
well fed and ornamented,
face painted over,
waiting
to be amused.

Richness:
the hymn on a Sunday morning
sung by a full choir and congregation,
the church, a series of vaults and spires,
carved, colored,
lofting high,
the space enclosed,
sacred and deep.
Outside
the sun is still warm
but the light begins to whisper
of winter.

Rich:
the song
and the silence
just after.

The Journey

May your journey be rich
and meaningful.
Not easy—
easy is not the point.

May you learn much
and be certain of little,
allowing yourself to walk a path
that sometimes has no footprints
ahead of yours.

Keep going.
The rules are simple, I think:
notice,
care,
appreciate.

Go slow sometimes
so you can go deep.
Seek
and savor.

Find what is yours to do in the world,
the exact dead-center place
that uses all of you.

And then do it.

CPSIA information can be obtained
at www.ICGtesting.com
Printed in the USA
LVHW111516240922
729195LV00005B/155

9 781630 519957